# I Love
# Therefore
# I Am

## by Peter McWilliams

Cover design by Paul LeBus
Interior design by Victoria Marine

Published by
Prelude Press
8165 Mannix Drive
Los Angeles, California 90046
213-650-9571

Other books by Peter McWilliams:

## POETRY

*Come Love with Me and Be My Life*
*For Lovers and No Others*
*The Hard Stuff: Love*
*Love: An Experience Of*
*Love Is Yes*
*Come To My Senses*
*Catch Me with Your Smile*
*I Marry You Because...*

## PERSONAL GROWTH

*How to Survive The Loss of a Love*
(with Melba Colgrove, Ph.D.
and Harold Bloomfield, M.D.)

*You Can't Afford the Luxury
of a Negative Thought*
(with John-Roger)

## COMPUTERS

*The Personal Computer Book*

Published by and available from

Prelude Press
8165 Mannix Drive
Los Angeles, California 90046
213-650-9571

# I Love
# Therefore
# I Am

# ONE

I love
therefore
I am

trying.

The rain-washed air
enters through an
open window.

The smell is beauty.

My pain-washed mind
tells me how good
it would be to have
someone to share
this moment with.

The feel is lonely.

My soul is bare
but no one's there

and the rain-washed air
does not care.

It's been two years
since we talked last.

You lead a church choir
somewhere.

The pauses between your
sentences are longer.
More pregnant — or so
you would like the world
to believe.  They make me
as uncomfortable as
ever.

"A person out of the past"
you keep saying, unwilling
to accept my present.

Questions answered by questions.
Statements questioned by silence.

Your ambiguity and my ambivalence
clash again,
for the last time.

We held
each other
and were
one.

I, ashamed of my passion

you, ashamed of your tears

we, parted.

To put it simply —

With you I am
capable of a full
mental-physical-spiritual
relationship

Anything less
would be a
mockery, and
would hassle me
beyond belief
(& beyond relief)

Speak now
from truth,
not sympathy.

When we are
together
we are
one,

when we are
apart
each is
whole.

Let this be our dream
Let this be our goal.

This pain I feel.
is it growth
or
destruction?

I do not know,

and that ignorance
creates more pain.

all I know
is that
I love.

$L$et's hope you
value your freedom
with me

more than you
value your
freedom
to
be free.

There you were

and I was moved

and you made the first move

and I was shocked

and you wanted to move in

and I was flabbergasted

and here you are

and I am happy

Within me,
you inspire
desire
contemplation
& creation

Is this because I
love you,

or do I love you
because of this?

# TWO

**I** love
therefore
I am

happy.

You accept me
for what I am —
even though you
don't know what
I am.

For this I
give you love —
even though I
don't know what
Love is.

All that is
pleasurable
will be our
domain;

the only
hurt will be
growing pains.

It's all new to me, too.
but I love it,

and you.

I am one with another
being,
and another being is one
with me,
Simultaneously.

and the ultimate outward
expression of my Joy
floods this sheet of paper…

not the words:

the tears.

I love you
for the love you give me.

You love me
for the love I give you.

I do not know who first gave
or who first took
or where it all began,

but I am happy that it did.

I am happy that it is.

I am happy as it is.

I am in short
in long
in love
(and happy!)

$I_f$
All
is not
One,

at least
we
are.

When I go deep
inside,
I like having you
outside

I missed you last night.
I missed you this morning.
I meditated.
I no longer miss you.
I love you.

My Hate,
where have
you gone
since I
met
My love?

When you are within yourself,
and aloof, and separated from yourself,
and thus parted from the universe,
and thus alone,

a force compels me to
use every trick I know
to get you back into
being.

When I have forgotten
what I know to be true:
that you are me and
I am you and we are all
and all is one,

a force compels you to
convince me that "we"
still exists, and that
"we" is better than "me".

A fabulous force.

I think they call it love.

The person I love loves me in return

I am a very happy man...

but I repeat myself!

d<sub>awn.</sub>

we swam
in the ocean

and we dried
ourselves on the sand.

we swam
in the ocean

and we dried
ourselves on the sand.

and we swam
in the ocean

and we dried
ourselves on the sand.

dusk.

I am loved.

I am happy.

I love.

I am.

Filling
holes,
becoming
whole.

Attempting
to be
worthy
of
each other's
caress.

Evolving
at the
speed
of love.

$O_f$
one
color
that best
describes
my love,

white

is my
choice,
for
white
encompasses
all
colors,

and
my
love
can
become
any
color
required
or
desired…

the red of passion

the orange of intensity

the yellow of happiness

the green of gentleness

the blue of tenderness

the purple of contentment

the gold of love


and
I am my
love's prism

# THREE

I love
therefore
I am

sad.

# CROSS WORDS PUZZLE

```
        R
    J E A L O U S Y
        J
C R U E L T Y           B           G O
        C               O           A
        T               R           M
        I N D I F F E R E N C E     S
        O       N       D           S
P A I N         G       O
                R       M
                A
                T
            L I E S
                T   O
                U
    A           D                 N
    L   O   H E S I T A T I O N
    O   V   A           P
R E S E N T   T           A
    R   R   E           T
                    W H Y
                        Y
```

How many more times will
tears be my only comfort?

How many times will I see
that the potential is dead,
and that "our" love was
really in my head?

How many more times will
I give up,

and how many times will I
want you so bad that nothing
seems good?

How many times with you?
How many times
with how many
others?

$P$eople
don't seem
to be ready
for the truth,
so here I am,
again,
on the
outside
looking
yin,

I could have reached
my goal with lies,
like so many others do,
but that would have
made the goal a lie
too.

I offered you something
that I have offered but
to three other people in
my life — and something
that I will offer to very
few others:
me.

Rather than face the
situation and decide
whether or not you
wanted my Gift,
you

ego-tripped
and
hedged
and
led me on & on & on
and
milked the situation
for all I was worth...

And during your indecisive weeks,
the voices inside me had a civil war:

One side said:
"It will be yes.
Love!"

The other said:
"It will be no.
Get the hell out
you fool!"

It is my sad duty to report to
you, myself & the world that
the "other side" has won.

The love in me is dead.

I feel empty.

Angry but silent and
walking away,

this will be your last
memory of me.

Hitching and freezing
in an autumn rain,

this will be your last
memory of Michigan.

I hope Atlanta or New Orleans
or San Francisco will be
warmer to you this winter
than I could have been.

So
this love
has gone

And the
pain
remains.

But this wound
will heal
— eventually —
and all I'll have
to show is another
bit of
scar tissue
on my
heart.

Someday I will
categorize
the
circle of pain
I put myself through
every time I get
hung up in someone.

I'll have a lot of time
to do it, too.

The insomnia's beginning.

with you comes the pain that makes me long for solitude. with solitude comes the loneliness that makes me long for you.

This has all happened before.
several times.
the events.
the emotions.
the frustrations.
the goddam pain.

only the other person is different.
but not by much.

it's all the same
and there's so much pain
ahead.

is there any escape?

is there anything to escape to?

This season is called
fall
because everything
nature builds
all summer long
falls
apart.

Like our love.

# BOYCOTT SOUR GRAPES

Hold on to your hopes
my friend;
hold onto your dreams.

Squeeze them in your
hand until blood
runs from them in trickles
onto the floor.

But what if your dreams have
no blood? What if your dreams
are made of clay or
cotton candy or gossamer wings?
What can I tell you to do
with them then?

Well, whatever they're made of,
and whatever you do, don't offer
these dreams to anybody —
because I offered mine to
some body (you) once and that
some body (you) turned them into
rocks and threw them back at me
from behind their (your) wall,
and I hope if this ever happens
to you, you will write a better
poem about it than I just have.

The promises
of your
eyes
were
lies.

Why must I
always fall for

chicken shits
on
ego trips?

You'll have no trouble
finding some sexy *homo sapien,*
(in) complete with a well proportioned
body
and a kind undefined minding
mind.

And together you can find:
the grooviest of movies and
a line of friends that never ends and
drinks and drugs and
lots of perfectly wonderful parties.

And one day you two may become three:
you, he, and your color TV.

But I'm looking for more,
and since you're not,

I won't be looking for You anymore.

To lose you as a
love
was painful.

To lose you as a
friend
is equally painful.

But lost you are.

The walls are sooo high,
and that finely honed saber
I had when I began storming
your citadel isn't even
sharp enough to
slash my wrists.

It's not that I don't care.

It's just that I can't
let myself
care any more.

My conscience is clear,
which is more than I can
say for my consciousness.

I tried.

I tried honestly.
I tried intently.
I tried, I tried.
I cried, I died.

It didn't work because
some part of you
didn't want it to work.

You need love, but not mine.

You need to love, but not me.

And I know that it is truly over
because I find more relief in
these "goodbye" lines than pain.

Fair well.

For me
it will be
easy;

all I have
to do is
find a
love-object.

For you
it will be
more difficult;

you have to
find love.

```
                die
                die
                die
                Die
                Die
                DIe
                DIe
                DIe
                DIE
                DIE
                DIE
                DIE
                dIE
                dIE
                dIE
                diE
                diE
                diE
                die
                die
                die
               d ie
               d i e
               d i e
              d  i  e
              d i  e
              d  i  e
              d   i   e

                dead
```

Understanding
has destroyed
my power to
hate,

but it has not
destroyed the
hate.

I am without a
love object,

but not without
love.

So,

Outletless me
writes poetry.

I hope you find a friend.

I was yours.

I hope you find a love.

you were mine.